Agringada:

Like a gringa, like a foreigner

AGRINGADA: LIKE A GRINGA, LIKE A FOREIGNER

Tariro Ndoro

 modjaji books

Agringada:
Like a Gringa, Like a Foreigner

Publication © Modjaji Books 2019

Text © Tariro Ndoro 2019
First published in 2019 by Modjaji Books
modjajibooks.co.za
ISBN 978-1-928215-76-9
e-book ISBN 978-1-928215-77-6
Edited by Francine Simon
Cover art, design and typesetting: Megan Ross

Set in Crimson Text

Some of these poems have been previously published in or by
*New Contrast, New Coin Poetry, Kotaz, Poetry International
Website, Kalahari Review, Oxford Poetry*, and *Thyini*

CONTENTS

Winter

†

Summer

†

Spring

†

Autumn

I long to join thy song but I have no voice

Rabindranath Tagore

WINTER

agringada *adj.* ~~resembling a gringa~~ resembling a
foreigner

In a place where erasure is mandatory, memory is insurrection.

Severing

After George Abraham

[adieu/au revoir] ə'dju,   French, farewell
                  ə_ rə'vwa,   French, see you later

When your mother says goodbye, she means [   ].
When you wave back, you say goodbye meaning

[   ] because you know you'll see her later today/not for
another five months.

You leave your mother where you leave your tongue, where
you leave your [   ] in the hostel car park, watching her car
turn to a pinpoint in a cloud of raised dust

Phantom limb pain – when amputees feel pain in hands and
feet that [   ]. You hear her voice calling your name at
night. She isn't there in the mornings.

You are six years old

The people in my pelt

I feel most colored when thrown up against a sharp white background
        – Zora Neale Hurston

the people in my pelt
wear floral uniforms with matching doeks
rock sleeping white babies in expensive prams
while the mothers sit in pta meetings,
sit near hockey fields, cricket fields
smoking madisons, cheering their older kids on

the people in my pelt work in gangs
blue overalls and black gumboots
they grade the land into neat green fields
using an iron roller, they answer to names
like lance and john uttered by mouths
that are decades younger than theirs

the people in my pelt move in silence
one man, a teacher, comes in weekly
wears a frayed suit, his cataract blue eyes
swimming in old age to teach a required language
mangwanani vana, the call
mangwanani vabepswa,
twenty four wooden voices respond
in grade four we were still learning *amai nababa*

the people in my pelt move with fear
I try to appease mean Mrs ████

who tells me not to act like a person
from the compound or something
when she catches me horsing around

my friend, Lorraine, dark like night
tells everyone her father is white

Cecelia

where have you gone to, Cecelia,
and where is your work dress,
familiar and
shapeless as sunrise?

who shall weave tales
standing by the bathroom mirrors
with a cleaning rag in one hand
and laughter in the other?

how now shall I sneak off
and sit on the gravel stones
outside the kitchen, listening
to joy if you are not there sitting
at three pm with your afternoon tea?

whom shall I wave at
when four thirty strikes
and you are not walking
with your friends shouting
goodbye?

self portrait at nine

You and Lorraine
are the only black girls
in the class photo
which is taken before
the taking of the farms

girls your age
are mad about gymkhana and
The Vengaboys
(no equivalents in your culture)

your grandma wants to know
why it is that almost holonyms
tend to trip you up:
>   *motsi/ mutsa*
>   *nzara/ nzwara*
>   *dzungu/ nzungu*

a cousin laughs at your syntax but
you do not tell her
that Sister sometimes
sits in detention
for speaking the wrong language
at the wrong time
that you are cultural chimaeras
who've forgotten the sound of home

You know your father through a broad scroll
on postcards with pictures of waterfalls

of Serengetis of white beach sands
signed and scented with Hugo Boss
Mother remains a familiar voice
at the other end of a telephone line
static like an electronic umbilical cord

You wear silence
sitting on the concrete floor of a library
a shroud like speech

Language does not belong to you

Detention Excerpt

The tongue that is forbidden is your own mother tongue.
  – Theresa Hyak Kyung Cha

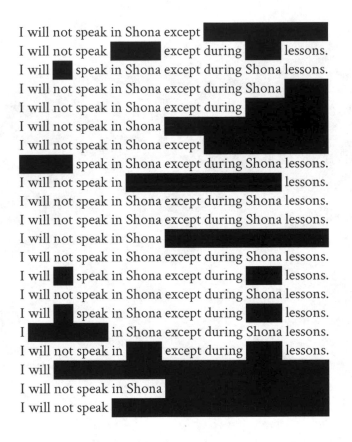

I will not speak in Shona except ▮▮▮▮▮
I will not speak ▮▮▮ except during ▮▮ lessons.
I will ▮ speak in Shona except during Shona lessons.
I will not speak in Shona except during Shona ▮
I will not speak in Shona except during ▮▮
I will not speak in Shona ▮▮▮▮
I will not speak in Shona except ▮▮▮▮
▮▮▮ speak in Shona except during Shona lessons.
I will not speak in ▮▮▮▮▮ lessons.
I will not speak in Shona except during Shona lessons.
I will not speak in Shona except during Shona lessons.
I will not speak in Shona ▮▮▮▮
I will not speak in Shona except during Shona lessons.
I will ▮ speak in Shona except during ▮▮ lessons.
I will not speak in Shona except during Shona lessons.
I will ▮ speak in Shona except during ▮▮ lessons.
I ▮▮▮ in Shona except during Shona lessons.
I will not speak in ▮ except during ▮▮ lessons.
I will ▮▮▮▮
I will not speak in Shona ▮
I will not speak ▮▮▮▮

Breaking a bronco

bronco (brong'kō), *noun* a western American horse
that is not perfectly tamed. [from Mexican Spanish:
wild/half-tamed horse, from Spanish: **potro bronco**
(untamed colt) from Latin: **broccus** (wild)]

1. walk quietly
2. don't act like a baboon
3. don't act like you live on a compound
   or something
4. act civilised
5. tell your mother I want that hair plaited,
   I don't care if it's relaxed or whatever

A

Mustang

mustang ('mʌstæŋ), *noun* an animal that strays [from Spanish **mesteňo** (feral, stray, undomesticated) (from Latin **mixta** (animals with unknown proprietorship)]

mestengo *noun* the girl who has to hesitate before she speaks because she must double-check that she is thinking in the correct language so that her words are not misconstrued. For instance, she must speak loudly in Shona or else, she is gossiping but when she speaks English, it must be soft and 'civilised.'

mestengo *noun* a girl of vague ownership: wild, adrift.
~~Belongs to you~~ but not entirely.

A

Seasons

february:

we all smelt new
factory hints of fresh cloth and plastic
ushered us into the year
there was, also, a reacquaintance with
hospital cornered bedding
and *lord behold us*

june:

frozen dew drops formed a white carpet
on the green lawn
we braved the cold in our ankle socks
and lace up toughies

october:

we squelched hunger with matamba,
which they called monkey oranges,
said we must never eat
they were also good for playing hockey with –
but you couldn't hit them too hard or they'd crack
spewing their orange flesh

october:

pythons crawled up from their
burrows and lay tanning across the road when
swimming gala day came the white girls
competed for the place of *victrix ludorum*
and we, t-shirt clad, graced the pool with novelty races

november:

we sang christmas carols
at the dutch reformed church
when they asked the girl
with the sweetest voice
from each class to sing a solo
in the candlelit procession
to the choir's pew
that girl was never me

Fragments: Weekend Mythos

pick a **colour** blue   the colour of ocean of water of vast expanses and perhaps   escape Rusape Dam rushing like blur before the girl's eyes to   the place where time stops still   home

pick a **colour** white   of white boats, white yachts and pillowy sails   of the people who swim there   the glistening of fishing rod twine where the girl wants to swim but she is told the river holds secrets   the dam is a crucible of ~~mermaids~~ menfish

and time stands still

       screams backwards backwards until Max the taxi driver brings her back to her grandmother's greeting "wauya mwana wa mwanangu, flesh of my flesh" and everything is like it was *before*

In the shadow of Tsanzaguru and the lion head Tikwiri

pick a **smell**   wet stones   of women hitching their skirts to wade in the river   of Perfection™ soap, greased onto shirts by women speaking freely   a dialect so rare it will be ridiculed out of the girl's mouth in later years

pick a **smell**, then, acrid (wet) cattle rushing to kick their feet in the dip   brown black mottled hides and curved horns an excursion soon to be outgrown, along with the climbing of kopjes

pick a **smell** acrid *dry* of the library her grandfather left behind shelves that still carry Hemingway & Emecheta   but zvipfukuto have eaten the pages   the plots have holes in them now   bags of fertilizer keep the pages company

pick a **sound** a clang   metal on metal   iron   sharpens   iron   cow   bells   on   beasts   coming   home as the orange sun sets

pick a **sound**   laughter   two sisters playing skip rope   in   the   dust   till   their   feet   are   brown   and   ashy on their tongues – a borrowed song that never made sense:

> *Christopher   Columbus   was   a   great   man/he   went   to   America   in   a   saucepan   /   he*
> *went   to   untie,   untie,   untie/   handy   over/   two   little   sausages   in   a   saucepan   /   one*
> *was rotten.../ and another went to die!*

into supper by firelight   orange flames and cricket song   wood smoke has burnished the walls   remember the girl of those nights   where the milky galaxy of bright stars shone sometimes blue sometimes bright and sometimes shooting across the sky   (make a wish! make a wish!)   then to gossip   and prayers   and an hour of radio one ~~zvizivise~~ announcements of births and deaths.

pick a **sight**   big silver old moon in the inky black night   hanging   like   low   fruit,   ripe   for   picking how   does   the   story   go?   old Rozvi kings   tried   to   steal   it   from   the   heavens   a legend as ancient as granite.

In the shadow of Tsanzaguru and Mount Tikwiri

pick a **smell**   wet earth   wet grass   early morning dew cow dung and clean smoke

pick a **colour**   pink   frock   Sunday best   follows her grandmother   her grandmother in Anglican blue in Anglican white in swift gait   a surprise baptism: glacial   water   on   the girl's   forehead   your   name   is   now   Theresa   Maria   Patricia   the   girl   forgets   her   new moniker

a particle,   **dust,**   gathers on the baptismal certificate   now folded   now carefully placed in the cardboard box labeled *Envelopes of Tudor*   wherein lies the last image of a long-dead grandfather   last seen alive in the summer of seventy six

cause of death: unknown

in seventy-six

...what we know of him: he was tall, I have his eyes, he was
a headmaster, he drove a car. the war was hot in seventy-six
(these are facts)

...concerning his death: he died in seventy-six. the war was
hot. he drove off one day, didn't come home. they found him
post rigor mortis. boys and men were disappearing those
days. the war was hot in seventy-six (this is hearsay)

...concerning my mother: she lost her father in seventy six.
she was eleven years old. she had two younger siblings. she
learnt to work hard. she learnt to work with the rains. she
sold peanuts by the roadside to pay for school supplies (this is
her testimony)

... she tells me not to speak to her in English: says she can't
understand it, she didn't go to school she says. I ask how
she helped me with homework? I taught standard 1 because
I'd reached standard 2, she shrugs. my husband died in
manicaland, she says he died in seventy-six (this is grandma's
testimony)

... the war was hot in seventy-six: in seventy six, manicaland
was hot. once there was a meeting called for in the bush.
turned out it was an raf ambush. selous scouts poured sulfur
on people. grandma crawled for kilometers on her knees.
entered her house through a window, waited for death
underneath her bed. the war was hot in seventy-six (this we
hardly speak of)

Mbare City Heights

1. Sekuru

I never met my grandfather. He died before I was born but I inherited his scowl, his scrawniness. Our name means luck – a conch in Mozambican Shona, a crown in Zimbabwean Shona, royal insignia. But he died threadbare. *Ane ndorochena* is "he who has luck" but when the white man came he had none. He who had been proud. Yet he was too small, too scrawny to be a black watcher or a soldier and so they made him a factory hand. Him, being a single man and a poor one too. Only Mbare City Heights could be his home. He died before we met. In the only picture I have of him, his eyes are not smiling.

2. Harari

You learnt to wash your body with soap in mouth,
Your panty too – otherwise it was stolen,
You learnt to buy a black and white TV
Even if you could afford colour
You learnt humility – pride made you a target

In Harari, your friend would steal from you
And tell you about it the next day
You learnt to walk around the slum by day
The flat – no cubicle – was too small for anyone
It was only meant for Pa
Pa the factory worker
Pa the quiet one

Pa who had left home in search for work

We had waved at him, all of us
When he left for Salisbury in the *Kukura kurerwa*
Amai had roasted a chicken for the journey
I never understood why he didn't send money
Those years of hunger…

When I too reached Salisbury
I understood
I understood what Pa felt
That Harari ate you
There was nothing to do there
Except complain
Get drunk,
Violent drunk
Wake up with *bhabharas*

You learnt not to judge a man
Starting barroom fights that were easier targets…
Than Smith
Than curfew
Than poverty
Than being called a boy when you were a man

SUMMER

con aguantar *verb* enduringly, with endurance

*eat the flowers on your table, drink the water in the gutter, nothing
grows anymore:
nothing grows, nothing grows*

Forecast

(1)

I stand at the edge of the last millennium
where dynamite fireworks crack the sky
in blues and reds and yellows and greens

I stand in platform shoes & discount skipsters
afraid
that the world will crash in a Y2K sequence
afraid
of a foreshadowed cataclysm
coming in flip flopping bytes
of catastrophic codex

But a small voice says:
The apocalypse will not arrive
in an octet of 1s and 0s
have no fear

the apocalypse will be ushered in
by a dirty storm they call Eline
it is possible
for rain to carry famine on its back
like a villainous hex
famine,

the word tastes more benign
than chewing that yellow maize meal
that is drought resistant

100, 011, 101
we'll record those hunger games in binary
we'll eat a meal a day in that dirty decade
tichaseva nemashizha emuguava

(2)

He carries his weight on a pair of crutches
three legs, one stump, a crocodile attack
Left half his leg on the wrong side of the border
when he tried to ford the Limpopo

but *my* hand was made strong
by the hand of some Almighty –
God

I'll live long enough to remember
some nine year old
peeking into a dark sky
waiting patiently
for an uncertain future to unfold

Home

Cemented yard
I hate it here
Ten steps from the gate to the house
Neighbours' avos in our driveway
Suffocating

Our house is even smaller than the yard
I never invite friends home
Sharing a wall with neighbour
Her rats infest our ceiling too

St Martin's

Mutsvaiii....ro!!
Tino-nama ma-po-too
Mutsvaii...rooo!
Tino-nama ma-poto

Street vendors with wares
no one wants to buy,
herald the second rising
of the semi-detached tenements

The first took place at eight
when working grown-ups went to earn:
when factories on the other side of Seke Road
began to pump smoke and fumes into the air

Vim yauya Viiim!!!

Now the dependents stir –
the man from next door
who always pops his head above our Durawall
sits on an old couch in the sun and smokes grass

Retired Mr Matthews takes a stroll
teeth still sparkling, swagger still sprite
Mr Matthews… who was forced
to join the Rhodesian forces in `76
because "Bobby from down the road
told the soldiers he was hiding"

Boys from around
wake up early to smoke,
linger lazily
at the corner of Winder and Adams

From across the road Tanya and his sister come out to play
their mother teaches Grade Sevens in Epworth
where girls fall pregnant before thirteen

Overhead aeroplanes make their way to the airport
Sometimes head out to Joburg
other times helicopters fly low
but we are too old now
to chase after them
screaming "aeroplane, aeroplane!"

Grace

This drought is not your first drought – you survived a famine eleven years ago, when you were barely a year old. When you suckled on a mother that should have been emaciated.

You survived because she willed it; she survived by the grace of God. You were born raising your fist to the world.

The doctor asked your mother: one must live, one must die. Which will it be? You both lived.

Repetition

After Sherman Alexie

1. Some things go on forever. 2. The rest keep coming back like a boomerang. 3. The moon moves in cycles, she goes to come back. 4. Sometimes waves are caused by the dancing of the moon, the earth and the sun, we call this a tidal wave. 5. Every decade the rains forget my country, we call this drought. 6. ESAP gave birth to my generation. 7. We suckled acrid milk from mothers who themselves were starving. They called it sacrifice. 8. A decade goes by and the moon, the stars and the sun move. Rain forgets to visit my home again. We call this famine. 9. The moon moves in cycles, she goes to come back. 10. Sometimes waves are caused by the dancing of the moon but these waves in my body give birth to blood. 11. Every moon cycle, the female body cramps in spasms, we call this dysmenorrhoea. 12. Sometimes the uterus bleeds so heavily, it almost kills its host, this is menorrhagia. 13. My generation learnt to speak in the shadow of kwashiorkor. This is a lack of protein. 14. Again, my generation moves towards starvation towards scorched earth towards oblivion. We call this pain... The moon circles round the earth and the earth around the sun like a boomerang and time pulls us back to swallowing heavy names of heavy diseases we could never quite pronounce no less cure.

Kudongorera guva

Without life and ailing he was borne
Up slowly by his son,
Up the red flight of narrow stairs
That led to that small flat we lived in
We set up his room
On the floor behind the old sofa
Of the one bedroomed flat
Where he lay day after day
With his sunken eyes on his medicine bag
"Mwana wangu anga adongorera guva"
Grandma would say, long after his departure
Long after the cirrhosised abdomen ceased to bear
Witness to a shot out liver

On moving to the semi-detached house
He came with us:
Took refuge on the scuffed red metal bench where,
Soaking in the sun, he ate porridge, gained weight,
Recovered
Spoke of the old days:
The hippies, *Black Mfolos*
Migrant miners returning with big hair, bell bottoms
And big boom boxes that blared shebeen songs at beer halls...

Then one day, returning from school I found him gone:
Knocked out by a common cold and leaving nothing
But a maroon knitted wool jersey and a silent son
Who neither mourned nor laughed

Pari

(Parirenyatwa General Hospital)

"Wait here," he tells us,
We've already been waiting for two hours
He types away, like he's busy working
But on closer inspection, I see he's on Facebook

They finally find a qualified person
To give my sister her tetanus shot
But first she must give him "lunch money"
(For services rendered)

We walk out, later
Past the haggard people queuing on the floor
With oozing bandages and undressed sores
Soiled cotton in red refuse bags line the corridor

Survival

...as in waking up at four am to hit the road as in road trip time watching the day break through a window as in norton, chegutu, kadoma, gweru, bulawayo, figtree, plumtree as in the dry stretch of barrenness between gweru and bulawayo must be metaphorical...

...as in dry riverbeds where water should flow it was an angry summer as in border queue at plumtree afternoon sun swelters as in warm conversation with cross border trader business is bad as in sitting on cement slab waiting on official stamps this is where lower back pain is obtained...

...as in sundown travelling through the kgalagadi brown lands flat for miles and miles, are we there yet? as in cheap takeaway supper chicken licken spicy soul food spread the blanket sleep in the car backseat no money for cheap motels as in two am rapping on the window copper with his black torch saying move along, can't sleep here humid interior moisture on the window pane...

Ramokgwebana Sketches

The queue (a human serpent)
Twists on concrete breeze block
Beyond cement slab seats
Strange man approaches

Purple shirt tucked in
Cap worn backwards
He acquaints himself with Mother

I've been doing this for ages
I've been around here often
This is how you do it
How to lie to border officials

Is denied entry

Francistown

So you're from Zimbabwe
> Yes
> Yes, we are

How often do you come here?
> Sometimes, always, when we're hungry
> when we've run out of groceries

How many of you?
> The whole family –
> import duty is cheaper
> when you travel as a unit

Where do you sleep?
> In the car,
> in the trailer,
> in the back of the truck,
> under the tarp
> we pray it doesn't rain

Really, how do you do it?
> We think of the hunger
> The bread queue
> empty shop shelves

When are you going back to your country?

Rites

Bud:

> Middle aged mamas *pakura* my first buds
> > with a wooden *mugoti*
>
> so they won't grow, won't attract men too quickly
> That doesn't stop aunties from poking, squeezing,
> from pronouncing, *"inga watokura!"*

Blood:

> In the supermarket:
> Mother buys my first pads
> In preparation for first blood
> I beg her to buy thinner ones
> that won't show through tight jeans but
> Mother was never one for aesthetics

Beau:

> My first beau is not as good looking
> As the ones in teenage movies
> He refuses to be refused
> He tells me I secretly love him back, deep down
> I'm just too shy to admit it

Media

on the vhs playing on the tv
the white baby outsmarts his black nanny who
lies sleeping on a chair, her body big, her lips red you
already know the story her name might just have been
mammy

in the wilbur smith paperback
the hero has a name like john adams
the heroine has a name like rachel moody
(her father was a missionary before he caught malaria)
the sidekick is a "big ndebele" they call him joseph but
his real name is unrecorded

in the cosmetic advert
there are three women
a black woman stands under a before sign
a white woman stands under an after sign, a caramel one
stands in between. in the cosmetic advert the shy girl has dark
patches on her skin.
she has no guy. they give her miracle cream. she uses it then
gets the guy. in the advert,
the lighter girl gets the guy

in the book i read
brave young boy races his horse to stake a claim
this is cowboys-and-indians frontier country
i long for open spaces where i too can stake my place
but i find all the stakes have already been claimed

only we are the indians. my grandmothers live on patches of
land
once called reserves, someone else laid claim
we are the vanquished

i sit in a memory
in a tub twelve years old
trying to wash africa off my face
– these are the days
after a man tells me i wouldn't change at all if a mamba bit
my skin *you're already the colour of nugget* he said to me

good [shona] women

good women gather round kitchens at family gatherings
discuss their men like it's a competition in victimhood

good women gather round kitchens at family gatherings
to feed men who sit at ease passing jokes and sometimes
flirting with women who are not their wives

good women carry their tusks in silence
spend hours bemoaning the state of drunken men who spend
their salaries on chapomba
        of absentee fathers who come home when they've no
        booze money left to spend
        of how they really ended up with the bruises they cover
        with foundation

good women carry their tusks in silence
gather round kitchens at family gatherings
bemoaning men they'll never leave
sometimes gesturing,
vasikana muri kuzvinzwa here?
musazowanikwa nemarombe
allowing their statements to hang in the air
amidst the smell of frying meat as we nod
as another aunty suspiciously adds
muzvichengetedzeka, girls
vakomana vemazuvano vanokutambisai

these good/respectable women who carry

purity like badges of honour
their bibles like shields
wait for nods of assent

but good respectable women
and their enemies vasingagoni kuzvichengetedza
end up in the same suffocating kitchens
feeding husbands they will never leave, even though
they have bruises from bumping into the kitchen cabinet

the iliad is wrong –
theogany does not hold the weight of the world on his shoulders
else us females wouldn't have to be strong
wouldn't be crushed under the heavy weight of these boulders

I live in fear

Of dark alleys and dodgy bars
Of being in a room with a man

Of the amorous boss whose money keeps me silent
And of the gangster whose gun will keep me from screaming

Of the husband who thinks the lobola he paid can atone for
my scars of abuse
Of the uncle who can get away with it because blood is thicker
than justice

Of the man on the street that can so easily pick me up and
drag me to an alleyway
And of the drunken men who will use violence

Of the bystanders who can hear all, see all
But refuse to save a girl's innocence

Of the chauvinistic man
Who can steal my innocence then make me feel shame

Of the society
That turns around and judges me

I live in fear of my weakness
His strength in silence

Crush

crush   (krvʃ),   *verb* to cause great discomfort, self consciousness
                         noun a tightly packed crowd
                         verb to subdue with great pressure

hot day. crush
hot day. sweaty bodies. crush
hot day. sweaty bodies.can't breathe.crush

a hand gropes me. crush. touches my body. crush
the pavement cops a feel. I look back at the daring eyes,
the granite wall of stony stares. crush. I cry out. who will
believe you,
sweetheart, they taunt? crush. I can't breathe. crush. can't fight
the pavement

take me. crush. take me back. crush. take me back to purity
crush

SPRING

alegremente *adv.* with joy

childhood is the sacred tongue you will never speak again

Painsong

(1)

numb me in epidural blindness
wrench scream and painsong and broken water
from my body
scalpel my stomach and ask me to choose
between self and infant

(2)

call me hope and place me in a bell jar
this will be a metaphor for things to come
even at first breath
these bruised lungs accomplish no greatness

(3)

first cry an hour before midnight
each breath a testament to new life

Single Mother

your heart beats steady
as I lay my head on your chest

you breathe deeply
and swallow

I remember, mama:

>   you sleeping in the lounge
>   with a knife in your hand
>   the day the robbers came into our home
>
>   you carrying me on your back and
>   Sister on your stomach
>   because you carried us alone

your heart
warm

your body
steady

Portrait of Maidei

After all,
I'm not the first to tell my man
to give the brat one of the toy guns he sells
so she won't tell the madam
we didn't go straight home
after nursery school

I'm not the first to yell,
Hey! Stop riding your damn tricycle
on the floor I just polished or I'll throw soap in your eyes!

After all,
I'm not the first to tell my brats
Go play outside while I run round the corner
just for two minutes to see a friend of mine okay?
Don't tell your mother I'll be back now now.

I'm not the first to get home after sundown
and arrive to madam's angry face and the brat's guilty face
I'm sorry I told

AUTUMN

con desilusión (adj) with disillusionment

*what is a word? a powerful thing. what is a language? a way of
saying ~~words~~ powerful things*

The offending document

It could be any handbag; it could be a messenger bag with extra-long straps, a designer bag with large Louis Vuitton logos or a scuffed black one that looks cheap. Let's assume it is the scuffed black one, it is the one you see most often. We must assume that its owner is stressed – that is how she walks, that is how her nostrils flare. Her hair looks frustrated, that is to say, it was once relaxed, and now it has growth; and since she's been hustled all day, the hair stands on one end. There is sweat on her brow and she is wearing a frock; yes, a frock because it is floral and black and made of cheap rayon. Her outfit is completed by knock-off tennis shoes that are not of the Tommy variety but she still calls them "matomi". Yet this woman is just like the twenty-something woman with dreadlocks (we pray to God she's not smoking mbanje). Her nose has a stud in it, another cardinal sin, and she too is frustrated. This can be attested to because she is telling her boyfriend, quite eloquently, on her iPhone.

It is true the older woman's bag is heavy because of the old Nokia phone she'll never replace, the one ply tissue paper still on its roll (in case she has to use a public toilet) and an old Fanta bottle full of water. Her wallet is just as scuffed as her bag but that doesn't deter her – most of her money is in her bra anyway. The younger woman carries a bottle of mineral water, chewing gum, a book and a passport. It is this document that has relegated them to the same fate. For now, the two women might share a camaraderie, a complaining together if you will, but after they've crossed the border, one will head for a bus station in Joburg where she will sleep under a truck for R2 a night until she has enough merchandise to sell at home, the other will take the Gautrain to Marlboro where her aunt lives and spend her days between Gold Reef City and Sandton. For now they are equal because of that offending document.

Cross the border by night

Cars will pass you on your way to Beitbridge,
You know they belong to your countrymen,

You will stand in a queue for hours
A semi-stampede will start up,
Reminding you of your asthma
You will panic.

A husband will go to the front and ask the officials
If they can please let his sick pregnant wife go first
They will tell him she must go and be sick in her own
country.

When you cross the bridge to the other side
The cars' headlights will illuminate the bodies
Hanging for dear life on the pillars of the bridge.
You will feel sorry for them:
If they do not fall to crocodiles,
They will be shot by farmers who think they are monkeys
No one will hear their obituaries.

In Messina you will be robbed
And it will be by your homeboys –
The ones who couldn't find a job here.

At the embassy they will hand you
application forms through barbed wire
You will not complain.

Instructional

After Allen Ginsberg

appease your countrymen whose way of life is remembering home in a
plateful of sadza
who walk to back alley takeaways where women with names like
Shuvai sell plates of sadza for twenty rand with a side of tripe
who look for Shona girls to pair with and walk in large groups for a
kind of shelter they never knew they'd require before
who pledge their allegiance to king and country in varying volumes of
sungura music and dancehall, the beats a whale song of calves that have
lost their way home

soothe these sons of the soil who are magnetised to your name,
surname, ancestry
whose tongues are not loose until they speak the language of their
fathers, conspiratorially and garrulously and sagely – holding onto
proverbs and metaphors that were redundant back home
who call each other wezhira, regardless of clan and totem and village
and name

sit with women who aren't above snubbing those who are not like you
in speech in ancestry
who won't allow you to speak with your Kenyan friend, "tinomenyeya
nerurimi rwedu asi imimi hamuna rurimi rwokuti nyeya narwo"
you've seen this episode before, you know the brutality of binaries.
No one knows you've been a migrant before the stamping of your
passport, like an epiphyte your roots are grounded in no soil, your
homesickness a perpetual flame that knows no quenching

your tongue does not belong to you, it belongs to homesick
brothers
who speak to you not as a person but as a beacon of hope,
something familiar. You cannot be selfish with it, not even with
older men who ask you how you are which village you're from,
when you're going back home; like surrogate uncles, not even
when they bare their teeth and pretend they're not married,
even then, your tongue is not yours

boycott   (ˈbɔɪkɒt), *verb* to sever contact or
association as a form of protest.

rejection   (rɪˈdʒɛkʃ(ə)n), *verb* refusal of an idea. (In
which our mestengo fails to absorb a new
language. She catches nouns but is too unsure
of verb forms to attempt full sentences)

when your tongue refuses to wrap around a language,
it is because:
       a. you are afraid to hear what they say behind your
         back
       b. you are self-conscious
       c. you're overly sensitive

when the teller in the shop gives you poor service after you
respond to vernacular in English, it is because
       a. they are xenophobic
       b. they think you're classist
       c. you're overly sensitive

when classmates speak over you, it is because:
       a. they forgot you can't hear
       b. they forgot that you were there
       c. you're not supposed to hear
       d. you're overly sensitive

A

Movies in Braille

To have another language is to possess a second soul
Charlemagne

1. Film actors

In the movie, a young Shah Rukh Khan sits on brown flagstones. He sings in desperation because he's in love with a girl from a rich family. He's too poor for her family. One of those old Bollywood productions from the early 2000s, where he's wearing a white Punjabi suit with sandals. Shah Rukh has aged since then, but you still feel most alive when you're watching Bollywood movies. As Shah Rukh sings about his girl in Hindi, you read the lyrics in white (sometimes yellow) subtitles, while his voice shouts down to you from the home theatre system perched above the mantelpiece. The parts you love most are the ones that don't translate exactly but being bilingual, you know what they mean. Words are just things that hover lightly above ideas.

2. Erasures, replacements

The opposite being foreign language movies with voice overs. Those over dramatic novellas on Telemundo where an unknown person speaks over the actor's voice. A vivacious young woman with a name like Yessica speaks but the woman speaking over her sounds sober and middle aged. You call the owner of this voice Harriet. You imagine, for some odd reason, pale toes and a ginger cat belonging to this voice – knitting needles and grey hair caught up in a bun. The sedate voice Harriet erases Yessica. The same way going to a private school erased you. There was a rule against speaking vernacular. There was a rule that said ~~black~~ girls had to have their hair plaited. There was a rule that said… well, there was a rule for everything. Even your name became homogenized, got skewered in all those white throats. They didn't roll the r's right.

3. Double Identities

To learn another language is to acquire another ~~soul~~ personhood. Sometimes you feel you have two separate souls? The English soul ~~erases~~ suffocates your Shona soul. In a nightmare, the one soul seeps out until only the other remains. Whenever a girl bleaches her skin, a native soul is suffocated. Whenever a Harriet speaks over a Yessica, a native soul is deleted. You imagine the day a nation full of souls is erased.

4. Liminal Spaces (refuge)

THIS DIALECT WILL NEVER BE SPOKEN AGAIN, a headline. Harrowing yes, but easily overtaken by global warming, the war on terror, stock markets plunging. But when Shah Rukh sings and you read the subtitles, both your souls are living – none suffocates the other. It's a sort of Braille.

LBD

After Kobus Moolman

because everyone else was going
because they were excited
because she was excited
because it was her birthday weekend
because she asked me to go with them
because she promised I'd have fun
because she promised I wouldn't have to drink anyway
because I went up to my dorm room
because I opened my cupboard
because I looked for something black and slinky
because they said we had to wear that
because it was the Friday night dress code at EQ
because the bouncers wouldn't let us in – (*if we weren't
dressed in black and slinky*)
because I had nothing black and slinky
because I couldn't afford it
because I looked in my cupboard anyway
because I really wanted the bouncers to let me in
because I was excited
because it was her birthday weekend
because I didn't find the outfit
because I went to tell her I couldn't go
because her face fell – just a little
because she wanted to go
because we were never close again
after that

Swept away

Fiela *verb* to sweep

Fiela *verb* to sweep [Sotho]

Fiela *verb* to sweep rubbish

Fiela [see also *murambatsvina*]

Fiela human rubbish clogs the system

Fiela am I different because of my visa?

Fiela what is the degree of separation between

Fiela legal rubbish and non-legal rubbish? Go back

Fiela to your country, *kwerekwere*, my friend said it

Fiela jokingly but I felt the sting // are we ever safe?

Fiela Jodi Bieber captured monochrome stills of prisoners

Fiela shackled in twos en route to deportation repatriation fields

Fiela I wanted the images but you can't take pictures in the gallery

Fiela Mother escaped with a mbare bag of her past five years, sleeps

Fiela in refugee camp at Beitbridge // says she has nowhere to go to but

Fiela government minister says disloyal citizens got what they deserved //

Fiela Black Easter sparked by lynching foreign criminal woman // exodus begins

Black Easter (reflections)

I say, each life matters
> you speak of liberty, emancipation
> & other Pan-African rhetoric
> but you invented words like kwerekwere
> & expected the necklacing not to happen

I tweeted *no to xenophobia*
> but words came before your machetes

Why don't you visit the townships
> my countrymen die there

It will be okay, that doesn't happen anymore
> but you don't know about the immigrations officers,
> about the wearing of long sleeved tees
> to hide my vaccination scars

How bad can it be, really?
> my cousin Farai made it his mission
> to be the hardest thug on the street
> so his neighbours wouldn't target him

How did that work out?
> it didn't

October 22nd

Camouflaged chopper flies
Low to ground
Cracks of stun guns

Joza Township is up in arms –
mob of xenophobic looters
Sweeps the length of Beaufort Street
No spaza is left unturned

High street retreats in shuttered windows
Shuttered storefronts
(Rumour says mob broke past police barricade)

Obliged, I ask my countrymen, how are you?
Where do you live, are you safe there?
But even then my heart,
Even my heart beats fast today
When I hear a crack of noise

Four Roads

Your winters bite me like an ugly scar –
Sheets of drizzle and confused
Weather patterns that summon winter
In the morning and autumn by midday
City of Saints, I am nostalgic of your call of artistry
Man who plays his brown guitar
At the corner 'cross from Debonair's and the scores
Of painters that tumbled through the July festival
eRhini, even moonlit
Brings me back to New Street clubs that spewed
Fighting couples onto tarmac – I remember, even
The drunken revelers that painted the town purple
In spurts of: throwing up, passing out, going back for more
Even those fake Samaritan boys who dragged
Inebriated girls to their res rooms
And called them 'takeaways'
Grahamstad, I grow nostalgic
Of High Street eating establishments
And even those gilded hair salons
Where white women were quick to tell us
Ethnic hair was not their concern
Remember those side alleys we danced into
That ushered us to Nigerian salons where our hair
Was not haram?
High Street.
And who could forget the statue of Colonel Graham
Still mounted on steed
Still claiming that land that should have been freed in '94
And the black cannons of settlers

that still frown down on the city, on the town?
And beyond the cathedral,
On High Street and Hill
Where a line of churches run down the line
Belying the liquor record –
Second highest consumption… in the world
Beyond the cathedral
English spoken in Afrikaans accents
Gives way to full bodied Xhosa
Those clicks I never quite learned to swallow
Down the road and right
To the Sunflower Hospice Shop
Where hipsters spent change on pre-owned novels
And the less fortunate bought pre-worn clothes
On lay bye
I am reminded of Beaufort Street
That vena cava that ran high in both directions:
The river of blue tar that transmuted
From hushed electric gates
And avenues of neat green lawns
Into a lesser tributary flanked by dust and garbage
On one side of it: the Grahamstown station
Where Muslim immigrants took refuge once,
When the city turned them out, bayed for their entrails
October 22nd, the date scored in my diary like a prison sentence
Beyond this point I go no further, unescorted
I remember that I too am not from around these parts
That this city, this town is not my own
Although I cannot erase it
From my being

Hyssop

"Purge me with hyssop, and I shall be clean:
wash me, and I shall be whiter than snow."
                    Ps 51:7, KJV

Wash me with hyssop, and I will be clean
                Kelly's Beach:
                my fascination is with the sound of the ocean:
                the rolling rushing waves, as in
                stuffing fingers in my ears and
                hearing the blood rush. my wonder
                lies with cargo carrying ships blowing fog horns
                in the harbour. love, let us swim in saltwater

                                    I will be clean
                do black girls have dandruff too?
                stray memory pushes to the surface
                must have been fourteen years ago,
                the smell of Heads & Shoulders™
                hot water, hostel showers;
                but it's the white beach sand in my
                hair that sends me there

Wash me with hyssop,
                sometimes a big wave knocks you out,
                sends you tumbling under water
                washing you onto the beach like seaweed or litter –
                life can be brutal this way:
                Storms River Gorge carries the broken dreams
                of the Eastern Cape's broken dreamers

and how many times did *you* try it?
there are no secrets here, did you ever succeed?

Wash me ████████ *and I will be clean*
        you have forgotten your family name,
        says father, let us sing of conches & kings
        he plucks a conch from the ocean
        asks if I know what it means:
        a spiral tattooed to the bodies of ancient kings
        he who has the conch rules them all
        and that is your name, he says
        that is who we are, my child

Wash me ████████████████████

        the wind and the waves and the Indian Ocean
        wash your soul –
        even floundering, even treading water,
        even spat out by a mighty wave
        with white sand granules stuck in your braids
        you are absolved, now, you are made clean

The dance of the mustang

but are you tired of apologizing
for being all the lines that tether you?
for occupying all the geographies that can't hold you?

remember this:
there are different ways to say a thing:
with hands, with faces, with song
I spoke with a foreign man once
I did it with my eyes
I said the word   and
Let it hover

they'll tether your tongue like they tether the geldings,
but you remain
                    unbroken mustang

see how other mustangs move?
they gallop
see how they gallop?
they run
and how do mustangs run?

With the wind.

Curse is
you will never fit in

Blessing is
you will never want to

GLOSSARY AND NOTES

The people in my pelt:
mangwanani vana/mangwanani vabepswa good morning
children, good morning Mr Bepswa
amai nababa mother and father

Seasons:
victrix ludorum a girl or woman who is the overall champion
in a sports competition
matamba kapenta

Fragments Weekend Mythos:
Christopher Columbus was a great man.. rhyme sung by
children as they skip
Menfish literal translation of njuzu (as used in Marechera's *House
of Hunger*) which also translates to mermaid, mythical creature
half fish half man
Tsanzaguru is a large plateau in Manicaland. The Rozvi wanted
to build to the moon from Tsanzaguru and present it their king
as a gift.
Zvipfukuto pests
Zviziviso announcements

In seventy six:
raf Rhodesian Armed Forces
selous scouts special forces regiment in the RAF

Sekuru:
blackwatcher black constable

Rites:
mugoti wooden spoon
pakura scoop
inga watokura! How you've grown!

Harari:
Before Independence Harari township constituted what is now called Mbare

Kukura kurerwa bus brand (to grow is to be raised)
bhabharas hangover

Prophecy:
Have no fear for atomic energy (and later, my hand was made strong) is quoted from Bob Marley's *Redemption Song.*

Cyclone Leon-Eline was a tropical cyclone that caused a lot of damage in Zimbabwe, particularly in Manicaland in February 2000.

takaseva nemashizha emuguava we ate sadza with guava leaves as our relish.
During the famine that occurred in 2003 – 2005, it was common for people to allude to the numbers of meals they'd eaten using binary. 001 being no breakfast meal, no lunch and one supper meal.

St. Martin's:
peddlar's cries: **mutsvairo** – we sell reed brooms, **tinonama mapoto** – we fix broken pots

Repetition:
ESAP Economic Structural Adjustment Programme, economic

reform programme adopted by Zimbabwe in 1990 to counteract national debt.

Kudongorera guva:
mwana wangu anga adongorera guva – my child had glanced at the grave (almost died)

good shona women:
vasikana muri kuzvinzwa here?/musazowanikwa nemarombe do you hear, girls?/ do not fall for beggars **muzvichengetedze, ka girls/ vakomana vemazuvano vanokutambisai** keep yourselves (pure)/ boys nowadays just want to play with you
vasingagoni kuzvichengeta who can't keep themselves (pure)

The offending document:
matomi tennis shoes
mbanje marijuana

Instructional:
sungura Zimbabwean music genre
wezhira term used to address someone from the same village
tinomenyeya rurimi rwedu asi imimi hamuna rurimi rwekuti nyeya narwo we can insult her in our tongue but you share no (common) tongue to insult us with

Swept away:
murambatsvina also known as Operation Restore Order. This was a large-scale crackdown against illegal housing and commercial activities across Zimbabwe to reduce the risk of the spread of infectious disease.
kwerekwere foreigner (derogatory)

mbare bag canvas bag, generally used by cross border traders

Four Roads:
takeaways slang term used to refer to date rape i.e. taking an inebriated woman home from a party/club

After this poem was written, Grahamstown was renamed to Makhanda.

ABOUT THE AUTHOR

Tariro Ndoro is a Zimbabwean poet and storyteller. Born in Harare but raised in a smattering of small towns, Tariro holds a BSc in Microbiology and an MA in Creative Writing.

Her work has been published in numerous international journals and anthologies including *20.35 Africa: An Anthology of Contemporary Poetry* (Brittle Paper, 2018) *Kotaz, New Contrast Oxford Poetry* and *Puerto del Sol.*

Her poetry has been shortlisted for the 2018 Babishai Niwe Poetry Prize and awarded second place for the 2017 DALRO Prize. Agringada is her debut collection.

†

LOS ACKNOWLEDGEMENTS

The original version of *Agringada* was written as part of my 2015 masters thesis in Creative Writing at Rhodes University, entitled *The Smell Hits You First*. I would like to thank Robert Berold and Joan Metelerkemp who worked tirelessly to guide my poetic aspirations and help me find my voice.

Thank you, Colleen Higgs for picking this book and to Aimee-Claire Smith and Juanita de Villiers for all the behind-the-scenes work.

To Francine Simon, who helped me whittle my manuscript into a book while taking great pains to keep my ego intact, thank you.

Thank you, Megan Ross, for the care and attention you put into making this book look beautiful.

I am deeply grateful to Mxolisi Nyezwa, Lesego Rampolokeng, Kobus Moolman for imparting their incredible knowledge about poetry and life.

I am also grateful to Batsirai, Chelsy, Tanatsei, Cynthia and Samantha, my Zimbabwean poetry group.

Thank you to James Arnett, Fouad Asfour, Tinashe Mushakavanhu, Stanely Mushava, JoAnn Bekker, Togara Muzanenhamo, Jane Morris, Philani Nyoni, Manosa Nthunya who have supported my literary endeavors in various ways.

Thank you Malebo, Mbali and Nelly for your constant cheer-leading.

My deepest gratitude to Tafadzwa, who has always believed in me, Kudakwashe who has always supported me, and my parents for their endless support.

Kea leboha.

Printed in the United States
By Bookmasters